THE DOMINIE WORLD OF ANIMALS
LIONS

Graham Meadows & Claire Vial

Contents

DOMINIE PRESS
Pearson Learning Group

About Lions

Lions eat meat and are called **carnivores**. They are the top **predators** on the African plains.

The largest of the African big cats, they are found in grasslands and woodlands. They hunt and eat many types of animals, such as zebras, wildebeests, and antelopes. Lions often **stalk** and attack those animals because they live in **herds**. This gives the lions a better chance of success.

Animals that hunt and kill other animals are called predators. The animals they hunt are called **prey**.

Their Size

A female lion is more slender and **streamlined** than a male. Adult males are larger and heavier than adult females. A fully grown male can weigh up to 420 pounds and measure up to nine feet from its nose to the tip of its tail. A fully grown female is shorter than the male and may weigh only about 310 pounds.

A male is called a lion. A female is called a lioness. A baby is called a cub.

Their Coats

Cubs have woolly coats with grayish spots. By the time they are three months old, the coat changes and resembles the hairy coat of an adult. The gray spots gradually fade, but they may still be seen on adult lions.

An adult lion's coat is usually a pale sandy, or **tawny**, color, with some white underparts that are often faintly spotted. The backs of the ears are usually black, and there is a tuft of hair on the tip of the tail.

The Male's Mane

The male lion usually has a **mane** that covers his head, neck, and shoulders. The mane begins to grow when the lion is about two years old. By the time the animal is five or six years old, the hair in its mane can be up to ten inches long. The color of the mane varies from light yellow to brown or black. Not every male has a mane.

The mane makes the male's face look larger, and it helps to protect him during fights.

Their Day-to-Day Lives

Lions usually spend the day resting or sleeping in the shade under trees. They usually lie on one side, but sometimes they lie on their backs with their paws in the air.

By resting for long periods, lions save their energy for hunting. They usually hunt late in the evening or during the night, but they will attack prey at any time of the day if the opportunity arises.

Lions spend about twenty hours a day either resting or sleeping.

How They Hunt

Lions often prey on sick or old animals, who are easier to catch.

When lions set out on a hunt, the females go first. They do most of the stalking and killing of prey. The males follow behind and come up to feed, once the prey has been caught.

Before lion cubs are two years old, and are able to join the hunt, they depend on the adults to share the food that has been caught and killed.

Only one in four hunts results in a successful kill.

Their Claws and Teeth

When a lion attacks, it uses its legs, claws, and teeth as weapons. Its sharp claws allow it to catch its prey and hold on to it. Just like a small house cat, the lion normally keeps its claws pulled in. The claws are **extended** only when they are needed.

The soft, cushioned pads on the bottom of its feet help a lion walk quietly while it is stalking its prey.

A lion sharpens its front claws only. The claws are about one and a half inches long.

Their Diet

Lions prey on animals as small as mice and as large as buffaloes. When they eat, they don't chew. They bite off chunks of their prey and swallow the pieces whole.

When they kill a large animal, lions often eat as much as they can. They can eat as much as sixty pounds of food at one feeding, after which they may not be hungry again for several days.

Males can eat up to a quarter of their own weight from one kill—a "lion's share."

Their Families

Lions live in family groups called prides. Most prides are made up of two to ten related females with their cubs, along with one to four adult males.

Each pride has a **territory**, which it defends against other prides. The size of a territory depends on the type of **habitat** in which the pride lives and the number of animals in the area that are possible prey. Territories vary in size from about 10 to 200 square miles.

Male lions roar to let each other know where they are. A lion's roar can be heard up to five miles away!

Their Young

A lioness gives birth fourteen to fifteen weeks after mating. Shortly before giving birth, she leaves the pride to find a safe place to have her cubs. Male lions are not allowed to be too close when the females have young cubs.

There are usually two or three cubs in a **litter**, but there can be as few as one or as many as six. A cub can weigh from two to five pounds.

Cubs are born with their eyes closed. Somewhere between three and eleven days after they are born, their eyes open and they can see.

Their Young

A lioness keeps her cubs in hiding for four to eight weeks. She sometimes moves her cubs from one hiding place to another, gently carrying each cub in her mouth.

Cubs can begin to walk when they are ten to fifteen days old. They can run when they are one month old.

The cubs are **weaned** at seven to ten months of age, but they remain dependent on their mother until they are about sixteen months old.

When they are fully grown, it is easy to see why these animals are often called the great cats of the African plains.

Less than half of all cubs survive to become adults.

Glossary

carnivores: Animals that feed on other animals

extended: Stretched outward; drawn out

habitat: The place where animals live and grow

herds: Groups of animals that have a common bond and live together like a family

litter: A number of animals born together

mane: Long, heavy hair

predators: Animals that hunt and kill other animals

prey: Animals that are hunted and eaten by other animals

stalk: To follow, or track, an animal

streamlined: Designed to move very quickly

tawny: Brownish orange to light brown in color

territory: An area that is occupied and defended by an animal or group of animals

weaned: No longer drinking a mother's milk; able to find and eat other food

Index